The 12 Step
Prayer Book

The 12 Step
Prayer Book

More 12 Step Prayers
and Inspirational Readings

Volume 2
Prayers 184–366

Written and Compiled by
Bill P. and Lisa D.

HAZELDEN

Hazelden
Center City, Minnesota 55012-0176

1-800-328-0094
1-651-213-4590 (Fax)
www.hazelden.org

Library of Congress Cataloging-in-Publication Data

The twelve step prayer book : a collection of favorite
   twelve step prayers and inspirational readings /
   [edited by] Bill P. and Lisa D.—2nd ed.
     p. cm.
   ISBN 1-59285-095-2
   1. Prayers. I. P., Bill, 1947– II. D., Lisa.

BV245T94 2004
204'.33—dc22

                                            2004047284

11 10 09 08 07   6 5 4 3 2 1

Editor's Note
Every effort was made to determine the source of each
prayer and inspirational reading included in this volume.

Cover design by David Spohn
Interior design by Rachel Holscher
Typesetting by Prism Publishing Center

Dedicated to
Margaret R. Graves

Contents

Inspirational Readings

Introduction

Prayer is seeking answers and direction in life. Meditation is listening for answers from a Higher Power and developing the faith within us to accept these answers. Reflection is the study of ways to change the answers we get from prayer and meditation into *action*.

This second volume of prayers and inspirational readings was written and compiled to assist all Twelve Step Fellowship members with their prayer life and spiritual progress.

Those who are just beginning a life of recovery will find help by working the Eleventh Step. Those who have time in the Program will find a deepening of their spiritual life. Anyone who has trouble finding the "right words" to speak with his or her Higher Power may find exactly what he or she wants to say in one of these prayers.

The suggestion in the Eleventh Step—"sought through prayer and meditation to improve our conscious contact with God *as we understood Him*"— asks us to *improve* our prayer and meditation life. May these prayers help you improve your spiritual progress.

This book, as with volume 1 of *The 12 Step Prayer Book,* is a companion to the meditation book *Easy Does It: A Book of Daily Twelve Step Meditations*.

Many members have learned, through times of quiet reflection, to work into their recovery life the answers their Higher Power has given them as a result of their active practice of prayer and meditation.

184
I've Found a Reason

Dear God, as long as my life was preoccupied with
my own problems, my own unwillingness and dark
moods, I was critical, insensitive, rigid, and defiant.
But when I honestly faced my defects and failures
and the worst was known and surrendered to You,
the whole nature of living changed. I am no longer
the emotional center of all things and no longer take
everything as personal to myself. I've found a reason
for all the suffering through which I have passed. It
is to be used in understanding and helping others.
Out of darkness comes light.

185
Happy, Joyous, and Free

I am sure You want me to be
    happy, joyous, and free.
With Your help I will no longer believe
    that life has no meaning and is filled with sorrow.
You, the Twelve Steps, and our Fellowship
    have shown me I made my own misery.
    You didn't do it.

I pray I will avoid the deliberate manufacture of
     misery.
But if trouble comes, I will cheerfully make it an
     opportunity to demonstrate Your wisdom and
     power.

Adapted from material in *Alcoholics Anonymous*,
Fourth Edition, page 133

186
Life Is a Gift

Thank you, God. May I remember during periods
     of depression,
The many times in my life when things *do* seem
     right, when I have those moments of clarity,
When I feel there is hope, when the sun shines
     down on me and warms my face, when Your love
     warms my heart.
I am reminded that life *is* a gift . . . this I pray.

Thanksgiving Prayer—
Native American

Great and Eternal Mystery of Life,
Creator of All Things, I give thanks for
the beauty You put in every single one of
Your creations.

I am grateful that You did not fail in
making every stone, plant, creature, and
human being a perfect and whole part of
the Sacred Hoop.

I am grateful that You have allowed me
to see the strength and beauty of
All My Relations.

My humble request is that all of the
children of Earth will learn to see the
same perfection themselves.

May none of Your human children doubt
or question Your wisdom, grace, and
sense of wholeness in giving all of
Creation a right to be living extensions
of Your perfect love.

188
Where There Is Charity and Wisdom

Where there is charity and wisdom, there is neither
fear nor ignorance.
Where there is patience and humility, there is
neither anger nor annoyance.
Where there is love and joy, there is neither greed
nor selfishness.
Where there is peace and meditation, there is
neither anxiety nor doubt.

by St. Francis of Assisi

189
I Must Change

Spirit of the Universe, I pray to remember.
No one can make me change.
No one can stop me from changing.
No one really knows how I must change,
Not even I. Not until I start.
Help me remember that it only takes a slight shift
In direction to begin to change my life.

190
Prayer for Natural Disasters

O God of Goodness,
In the mystery of natural disasters, we look to You,
Trusting that there is an explanation that will
Satisfy our minds and hearts.
Accept our compassion for our fellow men,
Our desire for their relief,
And hope and wisdom to accept
The forces of nature.

———————————————

191
My New Employer

I have a new Employer. Being all powerful,
    You provide what I need if I keep close to You
    and perform Your work well.
I have become less and less interested in myself,
    my little plans and designs.
Your wisdom shows me more and more what
    I can contribute to life.

As I feel new power flow in,
    enjoy peace of mind,

face life successfully,
become conscious of Your presence,
I feel less fear of today, tomorrow, and the hereafter.
I have been reborn.

Adapted from material in *Alcoholics Anonymous*,
Fourth Edition, page 63

192
Awareness, Acceptance, Action

Dear God, slow me down when all I do is try to
fix and control things and people. Help me to first
accept situations as they are when I become aware
of them. Slow me down in Your stillness. Mark my
awareness with unselfishness, my acceptance with
humility, and my actions with usefulness to me
and others.

193
Daily Surrender—No Regrets

This I pray, Higher Power: I will surrender to Your
will today, which brings me peace and joy that makes
all things new. I no longer have that trampled look
of someone forced to remember every mistake he or
she has made. I no longer hide under that blanket of
regrets. My daily surrender to You and the Fellowship
that surrounds me leads me away from darkness and
into the wonderful light of Your wisdom.

194
Thanking You for Little Things

I thank You for the house in which I live,
For the gray roof on which the raindrops slant;
I thank You for a garden and the slim young shoots
That mark the old-fashioned things I plant.

I thank You for a daily task to do,
For books that are my ships with golden wings.
For mighty gifts let others offer praise—
Lord, I thank You for little things.

Author unknown

195
For Guidance

Father of light,
Give us wisdom to know You,
Intelligence to understand You,
Courage to seek You,
Patience to wait for You,
Eyes to see You,
A heart to meditate on You,
And a life to proclaim You.

by St. Benedict

196
Teach Me

Dear God, teach me
   to listen to Your many blessings.
Steer my life toward Your will and the
   tranquil haven You provide
   for all storm-tossed souls.
Show me the course I should take.
Renew a willing spirit within me.
Let Your spirit curb my wayward senses.

Enable me unto that which is my true good:
  to keep Your laws and, in all my works,
  to rejoice in Your glorious presence.

Adapted from writings by St. Basil the Great

197
Happiness Prayer from West Africa

I am happy because You have accepted me,
  dear God.
Sometimes I do not know what to do with all
  my happiness.
I swim in Your grace like a whale in the ocean.
The saying goes "The ocean never dries up,"
  but we know Your love also never fails.
Dear Lord, Your love is my happiness.

198
Protected and Safe

Dear God, help me feel protected and safe today.
Free my mind from resentment, doubt, and fear,
    and fill me with love, peace, and hope.
When my faith in You and the Twelve Steps
    and the Fellowship is strong,
    I feel protected against the storms of life
    and safe in my mind and home.

199
For Loved Ones Far Away

O Great Spirit, Whose care reaches to the farthest
    parts of the earth,
We humbly ask You to see and bless those whom
    we love
Who are now absent from us,
And defend and protect them from all dangers of
    mind, body, and spirit.

200
When Our Hearts Are Lonely

God of life,
There are days when the burdens we carry
Hurt our shoulders and wear us down,
When the road seems dreary and endless,
The skies gray and threatening,
When our lives have no music in them
And our hearts are lonely
And our souls have lost their courage.
Flood the path with light, we ask You,
And turn our eyes to where the skies are full
    of promise.

by St. Augustine

_____

201
Make Us Strong—
Native American

O our Father, the Sky,
    hear us and make us strong.
O our Mother, the Earth,
    hear us and give us support.

O Spirit of the East,
   send us Your wisdom.
O Spirit of the South,
   may we tread Your path.
O Spirit of the West,
   may we always be ready for the long journey.
O Spirit of the North,
   purify us with Your cleansing winds.

202
Let Nothing Disturb Me

Let nothing disturb me,
Nothing frighten me.
All things are passing;
Patient endurance
Attains all things;
Whoever has God lacks nothing.
If I only have God,
I have more than enough.

Adapted from "St. Teresa's Bookmark" by
St. Teresa of Avila

203
Lead Me from Addiction

Lead me from addiction, in thought and action, to life,
From falsehood to truth.
Lead me from despair to hope,
From fear to trust.
Lead me from resentment to acceptance,
From hate to love.
Let peace fill my heart,
Let serenity be my goal,
This I pray.

Adapted from the Upanishads

204
I Ask Not for Easier Tasks

O God, I ask not for easier tasks.
I ask for stronger aptitudes and greater talents
to meet any tasks which may come my way.
Help me to help others so their lives
may be made easier and happier.

Strengthen my confidence in others
    in spite of what they may do or say.
Give me strength to live according to the Golden Rule,
    enthusiasm to inspire those around me,
    sympathy to help lighten the burdens of those
    who suffer, and a spirit of joy and gladness to share
    with others.

by Harry A. Bullis

205
Deliver Me from Fear

O Lord, I ask you to deliver me from
The fear of the unknown future,
The fear of failure,
The fear of poverty,
The fear of sadness,
The fear of loneliness,
The fear of sickness and pain,
The fear of age, and
The fear of death.
Help me, Higher Power, by Your grace, to love.
Fill my heart with cheerful courage
And loving trust in You.

206
Gratitude and Joy

Dear God,
May I write the wrongs done to me in sand,
but write the good things that happen to me in stone.
Help me let go of all emotions such as resentment
  and retaliation, which diminish me, and hold on
  to the emotions such as gratitude and joy, which
  increase me.

Arabic proverb

207
A Useful Life

My Creator, You have examined my heart
  and know everything about me.
You chart the path ahead of me,
  and tell me where to stop and rest.
Every moment, You know where I am.
You know what I am going to say before I say it.
This is too glorious, too wonderful to believe!
I can never be lost to Your Spirit!
I can never get away from my God!

If I ride the morning winds to the farthest oceans,
    even there Your hand will guide me,
    Your strength will support me.

Search me, O God, and know my heart.
Test my thoughts;
Point out anything You find in me
    that makes You sad, and lead me along
    the path of a useful life.

Adapted from Psalm 139:1–10 and 23–24

208
All Actions Are Born in Thought

I now journey in the realm of the Spirit;
Your wisdom has helped me be willing to change,
Your love has helped me believe I can change,
Your grace has helped me make the right decisions,
Your power has helped me take the right actions.
Today, this I believe:
All negative actions are born in negative thought.
All positive actions are born in positive thought.
Help me always to know this is true.

209
All the Good I Can

Dear God, guide me to
Do all the good I can
By all means I can
In all ways I can
In all places I can
To all people I can
As long as I can.

210
My Misadventures

O Lord, save me from taking the wrong road,
    save me from repeating my past misadventures.
I have learned in recovery that a truly satisfied life
    is only possible when I live the life You want me
    to live.
When I live with You in that secret place of the Spirit,
    I know I'm on the right road.
Your will (not mine) be done.

211
Continue to Watch

I have entered the world of the Spirit;
I will grow in understanding and effectiveness;
I will continue to watch for
    selfishness, dishonesty, resentment, and fear.
When these crop up,
    I will ask You at once to remove them.
I will discuss these defects with someone immediately
    and make amends quickly if I have harmed anyone.
Then I will resolutely turn my thoughts
    to someone I can help.
Love and tolerance of others is my code.

Adapted from material in *Alcoholics Anonymous*,
Fourth Edition, page 84

212
The Joy of Right Living

With bended knees, with hands outstretched,
I hope for the effective expression
Of Your Spirit working within me:
For this love and understanding, truth and justice;

For wisdom to know the false from the real
That I might lessen the sufferings of my fellows.
You are love, understanding, wisdom, and virtue.
Let us love one another,
Let us practice mercy and forgiveness,
Let us have peace, born of fellowship.
Let my joy be of right living, of doing good to others.
Happiness is for us whose happiness flows to others.

Zoroastrian prayer

213
For Protection

Grant us, O God, Your protection;
And in Your protection, strength;
And in strength, understanding;
And in understanding, knowledge;
And in knowledge, the knowledge of justice;
And in the knowledge of justice, the love of justice;
And in the love of justice, the love of existence;
And in the love of existence, the love of God,
God and all goodness.

214
Count Your Blessings

Count your many blessings, name them one by one;
Count your many blessings, see what God has done!

From "Count Your Blessings" by
Johnson Oatman Jr.

215
I Am Thankful For . . .

God, I am thankful for the people to whom I can
   relate in all situations.
I am grateful for all of them—
For those called "family" who provide community,
For those called "sponsors" who give guidance,
For those called "enemies" who help me see my
   faults,
For those called "colleagues" who share responsibility,
For those called "teachers" who instruct me,
For those called "helpers" who enable me to
   seek help,
For those called "comforters" who dry my tears,
   unafraid of my weeping.

216
Put Courage into My Heart

Lord, put courage into my heart,
    and take away what blocks me from Your will.
Free my speech so I may pass on Your goodness,
    so all will understand me.
Give me friends to advise and help me,
    that our efforts together may help others.
And, above all, let me constantly remember
    that my actions are useless if not guided by
    Your wisdom.

by Muhammad, founder of Islam

217
Honesty, Purity, Unselfishness, and Love

Dear God, may I breathe in the inspiration
    of goodness and truth.
Breathe in the spirit of honesty, purity, unselfishness,
    and love.
They are readily available to me,
    if I am willing to accept them wholeheartedly.

God, You have given me two things:
   Your Spirit and the power of choice.
To accept or not,
   as I have the gift of free will.

When I choose the path of selfishness, greed, and
   pride, I am refusing to accept Your Spirit.
When I choose the path of love and service,
   I accept Your Spirit, and then it flows into me
   and makes all things new.

Adapted from Twenty-Four Hours a Day, August 29

218
Support Me with Your Power

Lord, may everything I do
   start well and finish well.
Support me with Your power.
And in Your power let me drive away all falsehood
   so truth may always triumph.

219
Blessings by the Buddha

May every creature abound in well-being and peace.
May every living being, weak or strong, the long
    and the small, the short and the medium-sized, the
    mean and the great,
May every living being, seen and unseen, those
    living far off, those nearby, those already born,
    those waiting to be born,
May all attain inward peace.

Let no one deceive another,
Let no one despise another in any situation,
Let no one, from apathy or hatred, wish evil to
    anyone at all.
Just as a mother, with her own life, protects her
    child from hurt,
So within yourself foster a limitless concern for
    every living creature.

Display a heart of boundless love for all the world
In all its height and depth and broad extent,
Love unrestrained, without hate or hostility.

Then as you stand or walk, sit or lie, until overcome
by drowsiness, devote your mind entirely to this;
It is known as living here life divine.

220
Let the Worst Be Known

Lord, this I pray:
As long as I'm preoccupied with my own secret
problems, not sharing them with anyone,
I'm critical, insensitive, selfish, and full of self-pity.
Help me to share and honestly reveal my secret
problems.
O God, show me the way out.
Show me the way to make the worst known,
for then I will honestly release my secret problems
to those close to me and surrender them to You.
This suffering will pass.
This suffering I will use in understanding and
helping others.

221
Thank You, God

Thank You, God, for hearing my prayers,
    and granting my requests.
Thank You for the kindness You have shown me,
    and the good people who surround me.
Thank You for giving me this new life in recovery,
    and your great patience in helping me with my
    shortcomings.
Thank You for protecting me from the things
    that tempt me, and may my thoughts
    and actions demonstrate my gratitude to
    You.

222
Celtic Morning Prayer

This morning, as I kindle the fire upon my hearth,
I pray that the flame of God's love may burn in my
heart, and the hearts of all I meet today.

I pray that no envy or anger, no hatred or fear, may
smother the flame.

I pray that indifference and apathy, contempt and pride, may not pour like cold water on the fire.

Instead, may the spark of God's love light the love in my heart, that it may burn brightly throughout the day.

And may I warm those who are lonely, whose hearts are cold and lifeless, so that all may know the comfort of God's love.

223
Surrender to God's Will

O Lord, You know what is best for me.
Let this or that be done as You please.
Give what You will,
How much You will,
When You will.

224
Quiet Day

This is another day, O Lord.
I don't know what it will bring
    for I have not scheduled anything.
If I am to sit still,
    help me to sit quietly.
If I am to rest,
    help me rest patiently.
And if I am to do nothing,
    help me do it serenely.
For it is Your will
    for me to be comfortably quiet.

225
Carry This Message

Dear God, I now fully realize how much the Program, You, and other people have helped me. It is my responsibility to carry this message to those who still suffer, whether they are in need of our Fellowship or are in our Fellowship and are struggling today. You have demonstrated to me that life is no longer a dead end without hope. With this gift, I am now able to help others. My spiritual progress is measured by my positive actions. God, You have only asked me to be helpful and to leave the results to You.

226
Yes or No

Higher Power, today I will remember:
When I was practicing my addiction, I lost track
Of what was right or wrong, honest or dishonest.
Pride was defended,
Anger was justified,
Lust was accepted,
Gluttony was encouraged,
Envy was normal,
Greed was there to be satisfied,
Laziness was a way of life.

In recovery I have come to recognize and rediscover
The integrity in myself by simply knowing;
What is right is what I feel good about,
What is wrong is what I feel bad about.

This I make into a simple prayer:
I will continue to live by yes and no;

Yes to everything good,
No to everything bad.

227
May My Thoughts Be Guided

Dear Lord, You have guided me to demonstrate
    that common sense is the best approach
    to living in this recovery program.

The Tenth Step suggests it is wise to
    pause often and review all my choices.
My hurried remarks and actions lead to mistakes.
I have learned when I am wrong to promptly admit it.

From this I have learned
    honesty and humility.
From this I have grown
    in understanding and effectiveness.

Dear Lord, in gratitude I pray:
I am what I think.
All that I am comes from my thoughts.
With my thoughts and positive actions,
    I make my world.

228
Moment by Moment

Never a trial
>God is not there.
Never a burden that
>God does not bear.
Never a sorrow that
>God does not share.
Moment by moment
>I'm under God's care.

From "Moment by Moment" by Daniel W. Whittle

229
We Are Students

Dear God, once again, we are students.

In recovery we are learning the secrets of living completely.

In recovery we have cleared our thinking of obsessions, dependencies, denials, fears, resentments, and other destructive habits that have ruled us.

Dear God, through Your wisdom
  we have opened our minds to accept
  and our hearts to understand.

Dear God, in my troubled years I remembered
  my school days as perhaps the happiest of my life.
I thought they were gone.
But I've found them again through You, the Program,
  and my many teachers.
I love being back in school.
Thank You, God.

230
Blessing from Lao Tzu

Follow diligently the Way in your own heart,
  but make no display of it to the world.
Keep behind, and you shall be put in front.
Keep out, and you shall be kept in.
He who humbles himself shall be preserved entire.
He who bends shall be made straight.
He who is empty shall be filled.
He who is worn out shall be renewed.

231
Grant Me to Walk in Beauty

I come before You as one of Your Children.
See, I am small and weak;
I pray for Your strength and wisdom.
Grant me to walk in beauty and that my eyes
    may ever behold the crimson sunset.
May my hands treat with respect
    the things that You have created;
May my ears hear Your voice.

Make me wise, that I may understand the things
    that You have taught others in our Program.
I long for strength, not that I may outreach others,
    but to fight my greatest enemy—myself.

Make me ever ready to come to You with clear
    thinking and candid eyes, so that my spirit, when
    life disappears like the setting sun, may stand
    unashamed before You.

Adapted from a prayer by Chief Yellow Lark

232
Unselfishness

Dear Lord,
I must continually work toward unselfishness.
To be unselfish is to be useful.
When I am selfish, I am useless to myself, You, and
    others.
Help me to stop thinking of only *me*
    and to stop hoarding not only material things but
    also my thoughts and feelings from others.

Dear Lord, grant that I may practice what
    the Program teaches me.
My life has been saved by what
    others have given me.
I must, in turn, give it away to keep it.

233
Gentle and Soothing

Higher Power, what have I cried out for since my
    first breath, if not serenity and tranquility?
Only when I made a decision of surrendering
    to Your will did my life change.

I then made myself open:
To the gentle serenity of Your peace,
To the soothing tranquility of Your love.

234
Surround Me with Your Love, God

Surround me with Your love and guidance, O God;
I am not safe without You.
I am constantly exposed to this stressful world.
I am in danger sometimes of losing the battle to
    the very shortcomings of my own nature.
I can only surrender myself to You
    and believe that You will fulfill Your purpose in me.

I surrender to Your will, O God,
    even when I am beaten down by depression
    and caught up by my defects
    and my own appetites threaten my recovery.
You are my God, and You will not let me go.

Your love, O God, is an answered promise.
Your wisdom is an answered prayer.

235
May I Be Happy

I will sit down, quiet my mind, and connect
with that which is greater than my small self and pray:

> May I be free from fear.
> May I be free from suffering.
> May I be free from my ego.
> May I be filled with loving kindness.
> May I be happy.

236
Expectations

Higher Power, help me stop expecting so much
from myself. I set unrealistic standards, and when
they are not met, unhappiness follows. Help me be
true to myself and only expect what I am capable
of doing. As I grow in recovery and do my assign-
ments every day, I am able to do more. Your will
provides realistic goals. Your will provides what
I need to succeed.

237
Facing Indecision

Dear God, help me during the day when I face
indecision. Help me when I do not know which
course to take. I ask You for inspiration, an intuitive
thought, or a decision. You have instructed me
during these times of indecision not to struggle, to
relax and take it easy. You will provide the right
answers. This I pray.

Adapted from material in *Alcoholics Anonymous*,
Fourth Edition, page 86

238
What I Ought to Know

Grant me, O Lord, to know what I ought to know,
  to love what I ought to love,
  to praise what pleases You most,
  to value what is important in Your eyes.
Do not allow me to judge others according
  to the sight of my eyes only,
  or to pass judgment according
  to gossip,

but to know what is true and spiritual,
and above all to always pray for what
is good according to Your will.

239
Thank You for My Friends

I give You thanks, O God, for those who mean so
much to me. For those friends in the Program I can
go to anytime. For those with whom I can talk and
keep nothing back, knowing that they will not laugh
at my defects or dreams. For those whose fellowship
makes it easier to be good. For those who, by their
warning, have held me back from making mistakes
I might have made. Above all, I thank You, God, for
giving me all of my recovery friends who are bound
to me by a common problem; together we find a
common solution.

240
Use Me as Your Worker

Dear God, Your grace has placed me in recovery. You know how unstable and sick I was. Were it not for my surrender to Your guidance, the Fellowship, and the Program, I would have brought everything to destruction. I wish to give my heart and actions to Your service. I desire to teach Your message and be taught Your work.

Adapted from writings by Martin Luther

241
Easy Does It

Dear God, help me remember to take things slowly, for spiritual progress requires time for growth. Maturity is not an overnight miracle. Help me to be productive and keep me from procrastinating or being impatient and rushing ahead too quickly. I will remind myself today not to push myself faster than I need to go. I won't push the river; I'll let it flow.

242
Shinto Blessing

I humbly speak in the presence of the
Great Parent God:
   I pray that this day, the whole day, as a child of
   God, I may not be taken hold of by my own desire,
   but demonstrate the Divine Glory by living a life of
   creativeness, which shows forth the true individual.

243
Healthy Pride

O Lord, deliver me from false pride. Before recovery,
my false pride led to grandiosity, arrogance, egotism,
self-pity, misunderstanding, and fear. My misguided
pride was out of control, and I thought I knew everything. In recovery, I have learned my accomplishments
are not mine alone. I rely on the guidance of others
and faith in my Higher Power. When I indulge in false
pride, I close my mind, which desperately needs to be
open. Healthy pride in my progress, if coupled with
gratitude and humility, will not cause harm. Help me,
Lord, remove the intellectual false pride that blocks
me from others and the principles of our Program.

244
Reason for Hope

God of hope and serenity, I sing for joy because You have given me hope and serenity as I demonstrate the principles of our Program in my life. My world is sometimes full of problems, yet You give me reason for hope. I have come to You today to surrender my will to Your unfailing wisdom. Give me wisdom as I go out to my places of daily life. Teach me and guide me as I deal with problems, real or imagined. Thank You. Your will (not mine) be done.

245
Change Me—Ruth C.'s Prayer

Change me, God,
Please change me.
Though I cringe
Kick
Resist and resent.
Pay no attention to me whatsoever.
When I run to hide
Drag me out of my safe little shelter.
Change me totally.

Whatever it takes.
However long You must work at the job.
Change me—and save me
From spiritual self-destruction.

246
Blaming the Past

O Lord, help me stop blaming the factors that
I think contributed to my addiction: parents,
relatives, friends, the church, and most important,
myself. Help me realize that understanding may be
helpful, but blaming is always counterproductive.
The Program teaches that the reasons are not that
important. My progress and growth in recovery are
based on the spiritual. God, help me focus on how
Your Spirit, in me and through me, guides me away
from blaming the past.

247
Stop Fixing Others

Dear Higher Power, when I am overly dependent on others, I try to fix them. I have a real talent in pinpointing what is wrong with other people. But the very thing that enables me to see their defects most often blinds me to the same, sometimes even worse, shortcomings in myself. Help me stop fretting about others and instead focus on correcting my own character defects.

248
For a Sane and Sound Sex Life

Dear God, I pray for a sane and sound ideal for my sex life. I will subject each relation to this test—Is it selfish or not? I ask You to mold my ideals and help me live up to them. I will remember always that my sex powers are God-given and therefore good, neither to be used lightly or selfishly, nor to be despised and loathed. I must be willing to grow toward this ideal.

I will treat sex as any other problem, and ask You what I should do in each specific situation.

The right answer will come, if I want it. I earnestly pray for the right ideal, for guidance in each questionable situation, for sanity, and for strength to do the right thing.

Adapted from material in *Alcoholics Anonymous*,
Fourth Edition, pages 69–70

249
Quiet My Mind

Dear Lord, teach me to quiet my mind.
Stop my thoughts from racing from one thing to
    another.
Stop me from the obsessive thinking about the lives
    of others.
Help me rest and quiet my mind.
Help me let go of trying to control the lives of others.
Free my mind to be at rest.
This I pray.

250
Amelia Earhart's Prayer

Courage is the price that life exacts for
    granting peace.
The soul that knows it not, knows no release
    from little things;
Knows not the livid loneliness of fear
    nor mountain heights,
    where bitter joy you can hear
    the sound of wings.

by Amelia Earhart

251
Looking for God

Higher Power, I remember when I was new to
recovery I was told to go out and find You. I made
little progress until I realized, through surrendering
my will, You had always been trying to find me.
I then began to recognize the ways You are already
here with me. Once I learned to feel Your presence,
in my good and bad days, it became much easier to
trust You and to surrender to Your will.

252
The Miracle of Meetings

Thank You, God, for one of the great miracles
of Twelve Step recovery—the wisdom, insight,
and encouragement I receive in our meetings. As
I listen to others share their adventures in letting
go, surrendering to Your will, taking inventory,
and practicing recovery principles, I always hear
something that comforts or challenges me. Often
the meetings alert me to a problem I am having
and then give me hope and determination to keep
pressing on. God, make me ever aware that what
I do between meetings is what is really important.

253
A Summer Prayer

Long warm days . . .
The pace of life slows . . .
A time of picnics, and rest in the shade . . .
A time to celebrate the Spirit of Nature.

Father of Light,
    help me rest awhile in the cooling shade
    of Your presence.
Slow down my restless heart and anxious mind
    and fill me with gentle compassion for all
    Your people.
As the Program teaches me, this I pray, to
    "fit ourselves to be of maximum service to God
    and the people about us."

Author unknown

254
To Be Useful

Thank You, God, for I am glad to be useful,
    to have a reason for living,
    to have a purpose in life.
I want to lose my life in this wonderful
    Fellowship and so find it again.
I need the Twelve Step Principles for the
    development of the buried life within me,
    the good life I misplaced before the Program.

Thank You, God, for this recovery life within me
    is growing slowly but surely, with setbacks and
    mistakes, but still developing. I cannot yet know
    what it will be, but I know it will be good. That's
    all I want to know. It will be good.

255
Avoiding Gossip

God of Reason, help me be faithful to
    placing principles before personalities.
Before I gossip or find fault with others,
    help me remember to ask myself:

Is it true?
Is it kind?
Is it useful?
If I can't answer yes to these questions,
    I will not gossip.
Help me talk about principles, not personalities.
This I pray.

256
My Chosen Life

Dear God, help me live the life I have chosen and allow others to do the same. It's hard to live more than one life at a time. Keep me free from trying to organize everyone's life according to my plan. Help me turn over my self-assumed responsibility for other people's lives to You. Live and let live is the Twelve Step way of life.

257
My Family

Help me accept the potent emotions I may feel toward family members. Help me be grateful for the lesson they are teaching me. I accept the golden light of healing that is now shining on me and my family. I thank God that healing does not always come in a neat, tidy package.

From *The Language of Letting Go* by
Melody Beattie, page 117

258
Knowledge

God, may I not fear new ideas and the wisdom offered to me in my recovery. Help me keep my mind open to hear the help that is offered and leave judgment to You. I'm able to hear more clearly when I work the Steps and let You work in my life. May I keep growing and accepting the knowledge that comes my way. When I don't know something, I will admit it. Knowing that I don't know is also knowledge.

259
I Cannot Do This Alone

O God, help me pray and concentrate my thoughts
    on You:
I cannot do this alone.
In me there is darkness,
But with You there is light;
I am lonely, but You do not leave me;
I am feeble in heart, but with You there is help;
I am restless, but with You there is patience;
I do not understand Your ways,
But You know the way for me.

From "I Cannot Do This Alone" by
Dietrich Bonhoeffer

260
If I'm Discouraged Today

If I'm discouraged today, God of my understanding,
let me be able to give thanks for my recovery, my
health, my family, and my friends. If I'm discouraged
today, let me remember the sadness and problems
before recovery. Let me appreciate today and how

much better it is than the life I left behind. If I'm discouraged today, may I remember my spiritual journey is the sometimes painful process of learning to let go of things that are not important.

261
When Agitated or Doubtful

Dear God, as I go through my day I pause, when agitated or doubtful, and ask You for the right thought or action. I need to constantly remind myself that I am no longer running the show and humbly say to myself many times each day, "Thy will be done."

Adapted from material in *Alcoholics Anonymous*,
Fourth Edition, pages 87–88

262
Peace and Justice for All

Spirit of the Universe,
Lead us from death to life,
From falsehood to truth.
Lead us from despair to hope,
From fear to trust.
Let peace fill our hearts,
Our world, our universe.
Let us dream together,
Pray together,
Work together,
To build one world
Of peace and justice for all.

263
Make Me Brave for Life

God, make me brave for life: Oh, braver than this.
Let me straighten after pain, as a tree straightens
  after rain,
Shining and lovely again.
God, make me brave for life, much braver
  than this.

As the blown grass lifts, let me rise
From sorrow with quiet eyes,
Knowing Your will is wise.
God, make me brave; life brings
Such blinding things.
Help me to keep my sight;
Help me to see what's right,
That out of dark comes light.

Author unknown

264
Share Strength

Today I will stand up for those who are weak and
    beaten down, for those who are poor and treated
    unfairly, and
I will speak out for those who have no voice and no
    home.
I shall do this to remind myself that I was once one
    of them and could yet become one of them.
In doing this, I save another and keep myself
    from my addiction, my weakness.
This I pray.

265
Saving the World

Today may my prayers help me realize
I cannot control everything.
To put the world in order,
We must first put the nation in order;
To put the nation in order,
We must first put the family in order;
To put the family in order,
We must first cultivate our personal life;
We must first set our hearts right.

by Confucius

266
You Give Me Strength

Lord God, thank You for loving me
Even when I turn away from You.
I am grateful for Your constant care and concern.
Though I feel unworthy of Your great love,
I thank You that through my weakness
You give me strength;
And in my wanderings You show me the way.

Author unknown

267
So My Heart Is Quiet

Lord, I have given up my pride
    and turned away from my arrogance.
I am not concerned with great matters
    or with subjects too difficult for me.
Instead, I am content and at peace.
As a child lies quietly in its mother's arms,
    so my heart is quiet within me.

Psalm 131:1–2

268
Living in the Present

One day at a time,
This is enough.
Do not look back and grieve over the past,
For it is gone . . .
And do not be troubled about the future,
For it has not yet come.
Live in the present, and make it so beautiful
That it will be worth remembering.

Author unknown

269
I Am Weak

Lord, I am feeling weak—hear my prayer.
Lord, keep me from turning away from You.
I don't want to go back under.
Let me hear Your voice and feel Your faithful love.
I put my trust in You, Lord.
Keep me from my addiction; show me the way.
Teach me Your will.

270
Humble, Open-Minded, Willing

Into Your hands, O Lord, I praise this joy,
    this sorrow, this problem, this decision.
Into Your hands I praise each moment as it comes,
    each event You send to me.
Into Your hands I put this thing I have to do
    or suffer.
Into Your hands this love, this responsibility.
Into Your hands this weakness, this defect, this
    failure, this wrong thing that I have done.

And so, finally, into Your hands I place my life as
   a whole, all that I am; be it done according to
   Your will.

Author unknown

271
At Night

Day is done;
Gone the sun
From the lake, from the hills, from the sky.
May I safely rest,
For all is well!
God is near.

Author unknown

272
Faith Works

God, help me look beyond material things
And place my faith in the unseen.
For faith saves me from despair
For faith saves me from worry and care
For faith brings peace beyond all understanding
For faith brings me all the strength I need
For faith gives me a new vital power
And a wonderful peace and serenity.

Adapted from *Twenty-Four Hours a Day*, May 18

273
Mend Me

Lord, help me to right my wrongs.
There are so many years of pain and heartache.
I seek the words that will help to heal the hearts
    of those I have broken—there are many.
I must mend them without further damaging them.
Some heal with each day I remain clean and sober.
Others will take more time.
Guide me and grant me patience and sympathy for
    the ones I have hurt and want only to love.

274
Traditional Jewish Prayer

If my lips could sing as many songs
    as there are waves in the sea;
If my tongue could sing as many hymns
    as the oceans billows;
If my mouth filled the whole sky with praise;
If my face shone like the sun;
If my hands were to soar in the sky like powerful
    eagles
And my feet run across mountains like a powerful
    deer;
All that would be not enough
To pay fitting tribute
To You, O Lord my God.

275
Traditional Prayer from Mexico

I am only a spark;
Make me a fire.
I am only a string;
Make me a lyre.
I am only a drop;
Make me a fountain.

I am only an anthill;
Make me a mountain.
I am only a feather;
Make me a wing.
I am only a rag;
Make me a king!
To demonstrate my usefulness
To You, myself, and others.

276
Lack of Faith

Dear God, help me to stop demanding maturity
without the pains of experience and growth. It is
both unreasonable and impossible. I need faith in the
process to reach maturity. Lack of faith arrests my
progress in recovery. Procrastination and skepticism
are enemies of spiritual progress and attainment.

Skepticism demands evidence of God's help.
Procrastination prevents it. Faith, willingness, and
prayer overcome all obstacles and provide ample
evidence of God's help in our happy, clean, and
sober lives.

Adapted from *The Little Red Book*, pages 38–39

277
May I Encourage Others

Dear Lord, may I remember to encourage others,
    truly listen to what others say,
    encourage their expression of ideas and feelings
    by exercising patience and empathy,
    rewarding honesty and openness with affirmation.
You have instructed us to encourage one another,
    build one another up,
    be at peace among ourselves,
    always seek to do good to one another,
    rejoice always,
    pray constantly,
    for this is Your will.

Adapted from 1 Thessalonians 5:12–18

278
This First Step

Lord, I have nothing.
My addiction has taken my spirit and my sanity.
I have lost my family and my soul.
My life is no longer my own.

Help me to restore my life so it is manageable;
Make my pains bearable.
I cannot do it alone—I have tried.
Today I ask that You will be with me
    as I take this First Step.

279
Surround Me with Your Light

Surround me with Your light;
Penetrate the very depths of my being with that
    light;
Let there remain no areas of darkness within me;
Clear away the shadows of my ego,
    the clouds of my defects;
Transform my whole being with the healing light
    of Your love;
Open me completely to receive your love,
    and help me to let go of all that blocks Your
    healing.

280
Stop My Running Away

May I remain fearless and searching in taking my
daily inventory. This challenge has always seemed
difficult—difficult in facing myself as I really am.
I cannot run away from the truth or flee from my
wrongdoings. Higher Power, stop me in my tracks
when my misdeeds are chasing me. May I slow
down, stop, and turn to face them with the most
trusty weapon that the Program and You have
taught me: the honest truth.

Adapted from *A Day at a Time*, August 13

281
When I Question God's Will

There are still times when I feel insecure and uneasy
about my life. At those times I question Your will for
me. I wonder if I'm being punished for something
I have done wrong or I'm not working the Program
hard enough. I must hold fast to the truth that I am
just where You would have me. I must stop taking
control and attempting to force changes I'm not

ready for. This is when I lose touch with You.
I will be patient and believe answers will emerge
at exactly the right time.

282
The Four "A's"

Dear God, I have learned to live within my limitations and to live up to my capabilities as I grow in
recovery. As I try to practice the principles of our
Program, I will accept the truth that I seek progress
and not spiritual perfection. I pray to admit my
limitations and remind myself I am only human. I
have quit trying to play God. When I take my inventory and remember the Four "A's"—Acceptance,
Awareness, Action, and Attitude—I continue learning to live within my limitations and to live up to
my capabilities.

283
Part of the Solution

Dear Lord, remind me that when I was practicing my addiction, I traveled alone.

No relationship was more important. I was a hostage in a prison of chemicals. The Fellowship and Your guidance has broken that grip of isolation. I pray to remain grateful to the men and women who share their experience, strength, and hope. The Fellowship is a circle of spiritual vitality that energizes me when I'm willing to join hands. Alone I am the problem. Together with others, I am part of the solution.

284
Seeking Serenity

Higher Power, when I was using, I chased an elusive thing called serenity. My journeys outside reality brought a false peace. When I returned to reality, I found harshness and pain, which caused me to run back to using. Run, escape, pain; run, escape, pain.

Then something happened. My addiction wouldn't let me escape anymore. All that was left was the pain.

Recovery has shown me reality, not the problem. Trying to escape reality is the problem. Finding You and the Twelve Steps and turning my life and will over to You has created a reality of inner peace and strength. I pray and believe and trust these changes in recovery are necessary and good for me.

285
Fear No More

I will not fear those who have hurt me,
For You have given me power.
I shall sleep without nightmares;
You have given me peace.
I shall awaken with a clear and rested mind;
You have given me clarity.
I shall start my day happy, joyous, and free;
You have given me my recovery;
You have given me a new life.
For Your grace,
I will demonstrate my gratitude
In useful and positive action
Throughout this day.

286
God Is Our Shelter

God is our shelter and strength,
    always ready to help in times of trouble.
So we will not be afraid, even if the earth is shaken . . .
    even if the seas roar and rage,
    and the hills are shaken by violence.
The Lord Almighty is with us.

Psalm 46:1–3, 11

287
Our Faithful, Unchangeable Friend

How good is the God we adore,
Our faithful, unchangeable friend!
His love is as great as His power,
And knows neither limit nor end!
Our Creator, the First and the Last,
Whose Spirit shall guide us safely home:
We'll praise Him for all that is past,
We'll trust Him for all that's to come.

by Joseph Hart

288
A Triumphant Heart

Give us, O Lord, a tireless heart,
So no false accusation may drag us down.
Give us a triumphant heart,
So no hardship can wear us out;
Give us an honest heart,
So no unworthy thought may tempt us.
Grant upon us also, Our Creator,
Understanding to know You,
Persistence to seek You,
Wisdom to find You,
And faithfulness that we may embrace You.

Adapted from writings by St. Thomas Aquinas

289
Today I Will Trust

Today, I will stop straining to know
What I don't know,
To see what I can't see,
To understand what I don't yet understand.

I will trust that being is sufficient,
And let go of my need to figure things out.

From *The Language of Letting Go* by
Melody Beattie, page 205

290
The Weight of the World

O God of many names, bless You for lifting the
weight of the world off my shoulders. It was never
mine to carry in the first place. Surrendering my
will to You has removed the loneliness and isolation
that addiction placed within me. I need other people.
I need their help. The key to unlocking the many
gifts of recovery is asking for help. Your direction
and love has taught me to ask for help and to help
when I am asked.

291
Wisdom

Father of Light, You have promised
To give wisdom generously
To all who ask in faith.
Please give me wisdom;
Make me wise to know Your way for me,
Wise to make good decisions,
Wise to be useful to others,
And wise to understand Your word.
May Your Spirit give me wisdom
That I may know Your will,
That I may honor You
And find pleasure in obeying You.

Author unknown

292
I Will

Higher Power,
I will tell You the truth until I can tell others,
I will trust in You until I can trust in others,
I will pray for Your will and not my own,

I will not turn away from the addict who still suffers,
I will pray for mercy and not praise,
I will pray for humility and not righteousness,
I will continue to turn my life over to You
    so I may be restored to greater sanity.

293
Farther Along

Tempted and tried, we're often made to wonder
Why it should be like this all day long,
While there are other addicts using among us,
Never paying consequences though in the wrong.

Farther along we'll know all about it;
Farther along we'll understand why.
Cheer up my fellow travelers;
Live in the sunshine.
We'll understand it all, by and by.

Sometimes I wonder why I must struggle,
Go in the rain, the cold, and the snow
When there are many living in comfort
Giving no heed to all I can do.

Faithful till death, said our loving Master;
Short is our time to labor and wait;
Then will our toiling seem to be nothing
When we shall pass the heavenly gate.

Farther along we'll know all about it;
Farther along we'll understand why.
Cheer up my brother;
Live in the sunshine.
We'll understand it all, by and by.

Adapted from a traditional American hymn,
author unknown

294
Finding Home

Dear God, help me think of . . .
Stepping on shore, and finding it Heaven!
Of taking a hand, and finding it God's hand.
Of breathing new air, and finding it celestial air.
Of feeling invigorated, and finding it immortality.
Of passing from storm and tempest to an unbroken
    calm.
Of waking up, and finding it Home.

Author unknown

295
Release Hurt, Anger, Resentment

God of Reason, I am willing to release all feelings
    of hurt and anger and resentment.
Help me know true forgiveness
    and see each person as part of You.
Let my words and my actions
    serve only to honor You.
May my honest and positive action
    heal and comfort and harmonize my life
    and the lives of those around me.
Thank You, God.

Adapted, author unknown

296
Bad Day

Today was a bad day.
Forgive me for my anger toward others;
The anger was my own.
Forgive me for my prejudice toward others;
The prejudice and intolerance came from
    my own arrogance.

Forgive me for my lack of faith in You;
My lack of faith is my own fear of failure.
Tomorrow will be a better day.
I had a bad day, but it has ended.
And I am sober.

297
Forgiving Others

Dear Lord, if I am unable or unwilling to forgive
others for their actions, I will be unable to forgive
myself for my actions. The agony of resentment,
guilt, remorse, and shame will overpower me. These
emotions will halt my progress toward the comfortable and rewarding living we are promised in working our recovery program.

Dear Lord, help me to pray for those who anger
me and make me uncomfortable and those who I think
have wronged me. You have instructed me that forgiveness will always triumph over guilt and shame.
Remind me that my recovery is one-third love and
two-thirds forgiveness.

298
Reconstruction Ahead

My Creator, show me the way of patience, tolerance, kindness, and love. Help me to clean house and ask in my morning prayer and meditation for the energy for positive action. I have accepted the reality that there is a long period of reconstruction ahead. And yes, the spiritual life is not a theory; I have to live it.

Adapted from material in *Alcoholics Anonymous*,
Fourth Edition, page 83

299
Deep Peace

May God shield you.
May God bring you
   to the land of deep peace.
Deep peace of the running wave to you,
Deep peace of the flowing air to you,
Deep peace of the quiet earth to you,
Deep peace of the shining stars to you,
Deep peace of the gentle night to you.
Moon and stars pour their healing light on you.

Deep peace of God, the Light of the World,
Deep peace of God.

Adapted from an ancient Celtic prayer

300
Burden No Longer

Lord, take away this ache in my heart. I know I have
asked this of You before. This ache consumes my
every waking moment, haunts my dreams, weakens
my spirit. I pray You take this from me so the burden
is no longer my own, but ours together. I have wasted
enough energy and am ready to turn it over to You
completely. I believe in You and Your will for me.

301
The Grace of God

God's grace is a gift. Grace is the love and generosity
of God. Not until we felt defeated and made an
active surrender were we open to this gift of help
from our Higher Power.

I pray to receive God's grace in its many forms. It is the hope we feel after a good night's rest, the good feelings we get attending our meetings. I pray to stop trying to control everything and to stop missing the many gifts of God's grace. The grace of God surrounds me even in difficult times. Returning to that message renews my strength.

Adapted from Touchstones, September 18

302
A New Freedom and Happiness

Dear God, I remember the days that were controlled by my desires. The constant need to bow to the demands of my addiction. It made all decisions for me. There was a false freedom and a small bit of happiness. Thank You, God, for helping me work the first nine Steps of our Program. I am no longer a slave to my addictions. Freedom has come with abstinence, so has joy, gratitude, and love for others and myself. I have more work to do. God help me on my journey.

303
We Will Not Regret the Past

My Creator, by cleaning house and taking my
inventory, I have been able to honestly face myself
and stop hiding from the world and myself. I am
learning what kind of person I am. This is necessary
for maintaining abstinence and preventing a slip.
Without awareness of what the past did to me,
I cannot truly carry the message of hope and the gift
of recovery to those who desperately need it. God,
I pray to visit my past but never live in it for long.

304
Serenity and Peace

As I have entered the Realm of Spirit,
    after shaking the bondage of addiction
    through the love, encouragement, deep concern,
    and help from newfound friends,
    I've begun to know what serenity feels like.
Peace of mind is new to me.
Serenity becomes refreshing and comfortable
    as I realize I am free and able to make
    sound choices for my life.

That climate encourages serenity and peace.
God, help me to grow toward maturity, serenity,
   and peace of mind.

305
Benefiting Others

Dear God, bless You for bringing me from the
lowest depths of existence. What excitement has
come to me when I discovered I am not a worthless
human being. When I drank and used, I thought
I was doomed to be incompetent, unworthy, and a
dishonest person. No more. My escape from the
depths of despair has made me feel needed and
trusted. Others listen to my story of how I was, what
happened, and what I am like today. Lord, bless You
for making me a helpful person by sharing those
very experiences that made me feel worthless.

Uselessness and Self-Pity

Dear Lord, when I was deep within the bewilderment and agony of my addition, I often moaned, "What's the use? Nobody cares." I was a lost person. I thought I was incapable of doing anything worthwhile for anyone, including myself. Shame and guilt made me wallow in self-pity. By working the Program and focusing on positive things, I have changed. I have become more useful to myself and others. By recognizing my limitations and avoiding perfectionism, I've moved away from self-pity toward self-worth.

307
Losing Interest in Selfish Things

God, help me choose the path away from selfish things. I came into the Program an expert in dishonesty, deceit, envy, and grandiosity. Selfishness fitted me well. I was shameless in the ways I took advantage of and manipulated other people. Help me remember that selfishness and self-centeredness are a product of a sick ego. God, I must remember, every minute, that my reborn purpose in this new way of living is to help other people.

308
Self-Seeking Slips Away

Today, God, help me remember not everything is about me. When I was using, thinking of myself was my whole existence. With abstinence, I began to practice understanding, humility, gratitude, caring, and sharing with others. By having faith in our Program's recovery Steps and their other-centeredness focus, I am reminded that I am a person who truly needs other people.

309
Attitude and Outlook

God, help me to work on a positive attitude and outlook in my life. Help me adapt to the real world no matter how different and difficult it seems. During my addiction, I tried to escape reality and live in a world of fantasy. Recovery has taught me I can't change the facts of living, but I can change my attitude toward them. Today, I will learn new attitudes toward life's challenges and practice new solutions by working the Program. I'm learning to live in the real word with a healthy attitude and outlook.

310
Fear and Insecurity

Lord, continue to show me I don't have to fear people. When deep in my compulsions and obsessions, I was terrified of people, especially those who loved me. This new way of life has created a feeling of safety. My new friends, surroundings, and tools for living are lifesaving. Managing finances within a budget has produced far less stress. I pray for an attitude of financial responsibility in thought and action.

311
Instinctively Know

God, I pray the instincts that once compelled me toward addiction will continue to be redirected toward solving problems. By working the Steps, I have learned to face up to and solve the problems of everyday living that used to cause me to seek relief in my addiction. I trust I can handle situations with common sense and the help of my friends.

312
God Is Doing for Us

Dear God, as I practice patience, belief, and trust in surrendering to Your will for me, I now trust that solutions and miracles come in Your time, not mine. This Promise tells me I must accept Your help, not merely be resigned to it. I pray I will let go of my problems and turn them over to You with faith.

313
I Will Do the Footwork

Creator, my spiritual and emotional growth
    and the fulfillment of the Promises are not
    solely gifts I receive without any effort on my
    part.
I must earn the results by serious, dedicated work.
I pray to use the Steps as tools to do the work.
I will keep my mind open.
I will develop an attitude of rigorous honesty.
I will rid myself of denial and deceit.
I will let go of old ideas.
I will ask for help from my fellow members.
I will work on my shortcomings.
I will continue to make amends.
I will not be satisfied with half-measures.
I will follow spiritual instructions.
God, You give me directions clearly.
I will do the footwork; this I pray.

314
Happy Thoughts

Lord, remind me that the past is just that.
Protect me from my own thoughts.
Take away the old tapes playing in my head.
Fill my mind with thoughts of peace and serenity.
Lead me into the light, away from darkness.
Surround me with Your love.
God, remind me that yesterday is gone;
Tomorrow may never be;
Today is all I have.

315
Willingness and Action

God, help me remember that willingness without action is fantasy. I have left my fantasy life behind with my active addiction. The best way to get ready for action is to pray. Prayer makes me ready for success. Sometimes my prayers tell me to go right or left. Sometimes they just tell me to stand and wait for instructions. When I am willing to pray, I am willing to act. When I am willing, I am filled with prayer. Prayer always comes before action.

316
My Work Life

Today, I will pay attention to what recovery behaviors I could practice that would improve my work life. I will take care of myself on the job. God, help me let go of my need to be victimized by work. Help me be open to all the good stuff that is available to me through work.

From *The Language of Letting Go* by Melody Beattie, page 247

317
Accepting Every Task

Dear God, help me find the strength to be effective and accept responsibility. I am asking You for the strength I need each day. You have proven in countless lives that for every day I live, You will give me that necessary power. I must face every challenge that comes to me during the day sure that You will give me the strength to face it. I pray that I may accept every task as a challenge. I know I cannot wholly fail if You are with me.

Adapted from *Twenty-Four Hours a Day*, September 29

318
Unrealistic Expectations

Thank You, Father, that I have stopped undermining
my happiness with unrealistic expectations. I said
I wanted to be happy, but my past actions told a
different story. I held on to resentments because
I expected life to be fair. I expected to be given all
the good things in life simply because I thought I
deserved to have them handed to me. Thank You,
Father, for helping me get rid of unrealistic expectations. I will make fewer crazy demands on myself,
others, and life in general.

319
Sleepless Nights

Thank You, Father, that the longest night
    ends in dawn and a new day.
Thank You, that Your mercies are new every morning.
Clear from my mind now all black thoughts of the
    night and give me confidence as I face today.
Give me strength in my tiredness and the sure hope
    that Your love will guard and keep me.

by Lancelot Andrewes

Countless Gifts of Love

Now thank we all our God,
With heart and hand and voices,
Who wondrous things has done,
In whom His world rejoices;
Who from our mother's arms
Has blessed us on our way
With countless gifts of love
And still is ours today.

O may this bounteous God,
Through all our life near us,
With ever joyful hearts
And blessed peace to cheer us,
Keep us in His grace,
And guide us when perplexed,
And free us from all ills
In this world and the next.

by Martin Rinkart

321
Then and Now

That was then—when my heart was drawn to evil.
Every moment was a trap waiting for me.
Every word spoken was a lie and hurtful.
I felt only sadness and pain.
My eyes saw nothing but darkness.
My days were filled with despair and doubt.

This is now—my heart is filled with Your love.
Every moment offers new opportunity.
Words spoken are truthful and kind.
I feel joy and warmth.
I awaken to another beautiful day.
My days are filled with faith and hope.

322
Lord, I Bring Before You

Lord, I bring before You
The needs of my parents, friends,
Brothers, sisters,
All whom I love,
And all who have asked me to pray for them.

I pray that they may experience Your help
And the gift of Your comfort,
Protection from all dangers,
Deliverance from all sin,
And freedom from pain.
May they give You joyful thanks and praise.

Lord, in Your mercy, forgive all our sins against
    one another.
Take from our hearts
All suspicion, hard feelings,
Anger, dissension,
And whatever else may diminish the love
We should have for one another.

by Thomas á Kempis

323
Jumping-Off Place

O Lord, remind me of when I could not imagine life
either with alcohol or without it. I knew loneliness
such as few know. I was at the jumping-off place.
I wished for the end.

    The Program, the Fellowship, and my surrender
to You has shown me how to get out from under.

This new way of living has not consigned me to a life that is stupid, boring, and glum.

I have found a release from care, boredom, and worry. Life means something at last. My imagination has been fired. I believe the most satisfactory years of my existence lie ahead. Thank You, God.

Adapted from material in *Alcoholics Anonymous*, Fourth Edition, page 152

324
Help

Dear God, this I pray.
Help me until I can trust my own thoughts,
Encourage me until I regain my self-esteem,
Love me until I am able to love myself,
Protect me from my demons until I can fight them
    with You.

325
With Laughter

O God, as the day returns and brings us the silly
   rounds of irritating duties, help me perform
   them with laughter and a kind face.
Let cheerfulness overflow in my work;
Give me joy during my business all this day;
Bring me to my resting bed tired and content
   and grant me the gift of sleep.

Adapted from writings by Robert Louis Stevenson

326
Trust

Higher Power, when I was using, I trusted no one.
I lied about everything. Cheating was a way of
life. The only thing I could trust was my addiction.
When I discovered that was the biggest lie of all,
that was the greatest day of my life. Thank You,
God, for helping me put my trust in the Program,
the Steps, my sponsor, my group, and You, my
Higher Power. Little by little, day by day, I am

learning to trust again. And the greatest blessing is
that others are learning to trust me.

––––––––––––––––––

327
God's Power to Guide Me

I arise today
Through a mighty strength:
God's power to guide me,
God's might to uphold me,
God's wisdom to teach me,
God's eyes to watch me,
God's ear to hear me,
God's word to give me speech,
God's hand to guard me,
God's way to lie before me,
God's shield to shelter me,
God's host to secure me:
Against the snares of devils,
Against the seductions of vices,
Against the lusts of nature,
Against everyone who shall wish me ill,
Whether far or near, many or few.

by St. Patrick of Ireland

328
Live and Let Live

O Lord, we are urged to live fully, richly, and
happily—to fulfill our destiny with the joy that
comes from doing well whatever we do. O Lord,
it is more difficult to *let live*. This means accepting
the right of every other person to live as he or she
wishes, without my criticism and judgment. May I live
life to the fullest, understanding that pure pleasure-
seeking is not pleasure-finding, but that Your goodness is here to be shared. May I learn not to take
over the responsibility for another adult's decisions;
that is my old controlling self trying one more time
to be the executive director of other people's lives.
Dear God, help me to *live and let live*.

Adapted from *A Day at a Time*, October 2

329
Grant Me Your Light

Just for today,
What does it matter, O Lord, if the future is dark?
To pray now for tomorrow—I am not able.

Keep my heart only for today,
Give me Your protection today,
Grant me your light—
Just for today.

by St. Thérèse of Lisieux

———————————————

330
To Go Outdoors Each Day

Grant me, O Lord, the ability to be alone.
May it be my custom to go outdoors each day
Among the trees and grasses,
Among all growing things.
And there may I be alone,
And enter into prayer
To talk with You,
The One I belong to.

by Rabbi Nachman

331
Praised Be You, My Lord

Praised be You, my Lord, through our Sister
Mother Earth, who sustains us, governs us, and
Who produces varied fruits with colored flowers.

Praised be You, my Lord, through Brother Wind
And through the air, cloudy and serene, and
Every kind of weather.

Praised be You, my Lord, through Sister Moon and
The stars in heaven; You formed them clear and
Precious and beautiful.

Praised be You, my Lord, through Brother Fire,
Through whom You light the night.

Praised be You, my Lord, with all Your creatures,
Especially Sir Brother Sun, who is the day and
Through whom You give us light. And He is
Beautiful and radiant with great splendors and bears
Likeness to You, Most High One.

by St. Francis of Assisi

332
I Will Attend a Meeting

Creator, I will attend a meeting today.

I promise to seek out the similarities and not the
differences.

I will find something good in everything that is
shared.

I will praise the clean and sober and pray for the
using addict.

At the end of the day I will thank You for my
recovery.

It does not matter if the meeting was good or bad.

The most important thing is that I was there.

333
Patience for My Family

God, give me patience for my family members,

For their criticism and unkind words,

For their loud outbursts and often drunken ways.

Remind me of their kind words and support,

Their sober moments of tenderness and love.

Allow me to find the good that each of them possesses.

They are my family, and I love them unconditionally.

334
Wealth, Power, Fame

Dear God, I pray to remember
I will not care overly much for
Wealth, or power, or fame,
Or one day I will meet someone
Who cares for none of these things,
And then I will realize
How poor I have become.

Adapted from writings by Rudyard Kipling

335
For My Sponsee

Dear God, You have placed a new sponsee for me
to welcome to our recovery world. I pray that this
person will be filled with joy, peace, and serenity if
it be Your will. I'll try to help. I'm not a professional
counselor, medical consultant, or financial expert.
I hope to be this individual's friend. I have only
my experience, strength, and hope to share. I will
teach the ways of the Program and help this person find his or her own answers. I can't prevent a

relapse but can only carry this message—and help my sponsee find his or her own spirituality. I will listen and hear and learn from this person. I will love this individual until he or she can experience self-love—and beyond. Thank You, God, for this opportunity.

336
Happy Days

My Creator, take me back to my childhood,
When I was carefree and innocent,
When my heart was filled with laughter and love,
When joy surrounded me,
When I had no responsibilities, no concerns.
I give thanks for those memories;
I cling to them.

For when my life is spinning out of control,
It may seem that way for only a moment,
Sometimes for a day, perhaps an entire week.

Thank You, God, for the memories of childhood.
I remember them; I feel relaxed and relieved.

I remember I've known peace and joy before.
When all is spinning out of control,
I will know peace and joy again.

337
The Simple Things

Lord, I pray to stay uncomplicated and do well
these simple tasks:
If I open it, I will close it.
If I turn it on, I will turn it off.
If I unlock it, I will lock it up.
If I break it, I will admit it.
If I borrow it, I will return it.
If I make a mess, I will clean it up.
If I value it, I will take care of it.
If it will brighten someone's day, I will say it!

Author unknown

338
Direct and Guide My Journey

O Lord, direct and guide my steps on my journey,
    and let me travel in health, joy, and peace.
Keep me from traps and dangers,
    and protect me from any enemies who
    I might meet along the way.
Bless and protect my journey!
Let me win favor in Your eyes and in the
    sight of those around me.
Blessed are You, O Lord,
    Who hears and grants our prayers.

Adapted from a Jewish prayer, author unknown

339
The Strength of Humility

Higher Power, I have learned in recovery that there
is no greater defense against the cunning, baffling,
and powerful disease than a humble attitude. I pray
for understanding that there is strength and wisdom
which come from true humility. Humility has nothing to do with shyness, weakness, or putting myself

down. Humility is living in a proper relationship
with You. When I walk with You, I don't have to try to
be humble. I am humble.

340
Strengthen Me

Lord, I am an empty vessel that needs to be filled.
My Lord, fill it.
I am weak in faith; strengthen me.
I am cold in love; warm me and make me
    enthusiastic—
That my love may go out to my neighbor.
I do not have a strong and firm faith;
At times I doubt and am unable to trust you.
O Lord, help me.
Strengthen my faith and trust in You.

Adapted from writings by Martin Luther

341
Becoming Whole

Dear God, I pray my physical, emotional, intellectual, and spiritual selves become one, a whole person again. I thank You for showing me how to match my outside to my inside. To laugh when I feel like laughing. To cry when I feel sad. To recognize my own anger or fear or guilt. I pray for wholeness.

Adapted from *A Day at a Time*, May 18

342
Through These Doors

Dear God,
Please get me through these doors.
A meeting is what I need.
Remind me to leave my ego and intolerance outside.
Help me to hear the strength and hope in everyone's
    words.
We are the same but appear so different.
I will remember that others' experiences will help my
    recovery just as my experience may help another.

343
We Need Only Obey

Dear God, I realize the whole course of things goes
to teach me faith. I need only obey. There is guidance for me, and by listening I shall hear the right
word. I will place myself in the middle of the stream
of power and wisdom that flows from You; I will
place myself in the center of that flood. And then
I may know the truth, the right, and contentment.

Adapted from writings by Ralph Waldo Emerson

344
For the Spirit of Prayer

Help me, Higher Power, to cultivate the habit of
prayer. Enable me to know Your will. I pray I may
conform my actions to the demands of Your will.
I will pray with concentration of my mind, and I will
pray with all my soul. I will pray to You in words of
devotion with all my heart. I will pray to You aloud,
and I will pray to You in silence. For You hear my
prayers, even in thought, and measure my feelings

and know my aspirations. I will pray, O God, that
prayer may lift me to You and make me Yours.

Adapted from a Zoroastrian prayer

345
Father of Light

O my Father, Father of Light,
Who watches over us all,
I have no words to thank You.
But with Your great wisdom
I am sure that You can see
My willingness to change
And how I value Your glorious gifts.

O my Father, when I look upon Your greatness,
I am confounded with awe.
O Supreme Being,
Ruler of all things earthly and heavenly,
I am your warrior,
Ready to act in accordance with Your will.

Adapted from a Kenyan prayer

346
Better Relationships

I pray for the opportunity to form better relationships now that I am in recovery. The Program has revealed a need to completely overhaul my attitudes about intimate and personal relations. I pray the working of the Program will help me be a better partner in relationships. Most of the time I never really needed better partners. I just needed to be a better person.

347
God's Love

I pray that I may walk in Your love, God. I pray that as I go, I may feel the spring of Your power in my steps and the joy of Your love in my heart. A consciousness of Your loving presence makes all life different. You have brought me relief from the cares and worries of my daily life. I pray for the freedom and serenity of a sober life.

Adapted from *Twenty-Four Hours a Day*, September 8

348
God of Our Life

God of our Life,
There are days when the burdens we carry
Hurt our shoulders and weigh us down,
When our lives have no music in them
And our hearts are lonely.
Flood our path with light, we pray.
Turn our eyes to where the skies are full of promise;
Tune our hearts to brave music;
Give us a sense of fellowship with others,
And lift our spirits so we may encourage
Others who journey with us on the road of recovery.

Adapted from writings by St. Augustine

349
Power of Choice

Dear God, I pray for Your help
   in making the right choices.
I am, at any given moment of my life in recovery,
   the sum total of the choices I make.
I pray for Your guidance in choosing between

positive and negative,
    humility and arrogance,
    gratitude and self-centeredness;
And if at times my choices prove wrong,
    help me to learn from those experiences.

350
Procrastination

Higher Power, it was so easy to put things off during
my addiction. I pray to remember that postponing
facing up to reality is really self-pity in action.
When I procrastinate about solving problems, I am
only making the problems worse. Let me remember
that solutions come from taking action. I pray to
stop wasting precious time.

351
A Peaceful Pace

Today, God, help me focus on a peaceful pace rather than a harried one. I will keep moving forward gently, not frantically. Help me let go of my need to be anxious, upset, and harried. Help me replace it with a need to be at peace and in harmony.

From *The Language of Letting Go* by Melody Beattie, page 90

352
Fear

Dear God, fear used to be my worst enemy when I was locked up in my addiction. It prevented me from living fully. It kept me standing still. I now see how fear kept me a prisoner of my addiction and character defects. I will share my fears with You and others in the Program. I pray to work to get past my fears.

353
God Is Enough

Lord, I am grateful that when I got to the bottom and there was nothing left but You, I found that You were enough. My surrender and growing spirituality grant me serenity when surrounded with turmoil. I have an active concern for the well-being of other people. My spiritual growth has helped me, through my attitudes and actions, to better live with myself, You, and others.

_____

354
Thank You for Today

Good night, Lord.
Thank You for today, for my sanity, my life,
 for the people surrounding me, for fellowship
 and my recovery.
Tonight, I also pray for the addicts who still suffer.
 I pray that You relieve their suffering if only for
 a moment, a moment that may bring them closer
 to You and recovery.
I look forward to tomorrow and another
 day of sobriety.

Teach Me Your Will

Lord, take me from insanity;
Show me the way to serenity;
Remove my shortcomings;
Guide me toward forgiveness;
Remind me of my will;
Teach me Your will.
God, I ask that You love me until
   I am able to love myself;
Believe in me as I learn to believe in You;
Trust me until I can trust completely in You;
Be with me now just as You have been
   with me in the past.

356
To Grow and Blossom

Lord, I mourn the loss of my innocence. By sharing my experiences, I hope to recapture it. Lord, I long to feel more, trust more, laugh more, and live life fully. Show me the way, God. I thank You for my renewed sanity and my sobriety. When I have both, I can grow and blossom. Everyone in my family, the Fellowship, and my neighborhood can benefit from my peace.

357
Your Destiny

Watch your thoughts,
    they become your words.
Watch your words,
    they become your actions.
Watch your actions,
    they become your habits.
Watch your habits,
    they become your character.
Watch your character,
    it becomes your destiny.

Author unknown

358
Speak Your Truth

Speak your truth.
Listen when others speak theirs too.
When you let go of fear, you will learn to love others
    and you will let them love you.

Do not be afraid of dying.
But do not be afraid to live.
Ask yourself what that means.
Open your heart to love, for that is why you're here.
And know that you are, and always have been,
    One with God and all who live.

by Melody Beattie

359
Be Patient with Everyone

Be patient with everyone, but above all with yourself . . . do not be disappointed by your imperfec-
tions, but always rise up with fresh courage. How
are you to be patient in dealing with your neighbor's
faults if you are impatient in dealing with your own?
They who are worried by their own shortcomings
will not correct them. All positive progress comes
from a calm and peaceful mind.

From writings by St. Francis de Sales

The Four Absolutes

Absolute Honesty
Both with ourselves and with others, in word, deed,
and thought.

Absolute Unselfishness
To be willing, wherever possible, to help others who
need our help.

Absolute Love
You shall love the Lord with all your heart, and with
all your soul, and with all your mind. And . . . you
shall love your neighbor as yourself.

Absolute Purity
Purity of mind, of body, and of purpose.

by the Oxford Group; used by early AAs
before the Twelve Steps were written

361
Always Remember

There is no growth without pain (pain is not optional), so hurt a little bit.

There is no laughter without tears, so cry often. (Don't be ashamed to cry, for if you don't, you will be ever secure but always lonely.)

There is no peace without first knowing turmoil in the soul, so be at war with yourself sometimes.

There is no grace without first wrestling with guilt. If you are wrestling, let God's grace surround you and give you new life.

362
That Great Purpose

Keep making progress in your Twelve Step recovery.
Let your aim be as steady as a star.
Let the world battle and stress.
You may be assaulted, hassled,
    insulted, slandered, wounded, and rejected.
You may be chased by enemies,
    abused by them, forgotten by friends,

hated and rejected by others,
but see to it
that with steady determination
and with unfaltering devotion,
you pursue that great purpose of your life
and the object of your being
until at last you can say:
"I have finished the work which You,
dear God, have given me to do."

Adapted, author unknown

363
I Wish I Were

I wish I were big enough to honestly admit all my
    shortcomings,
Brilliant enough to accept praise without it making
    me arrogant,
Tall enough to tower over dishonesty,
Strong enough to welcome criticism,
Compassionate enough to understand human
    frailties,
Wise enough to recognize mistakes,
Humble enough to appreciate greatness,

Brave enough to stand by my friends,
Human enough to be thoughtful of my neighbor,
And spiritual enough to be devoted to the love
of God.

Author unknown

364
Be at Peace

Do not look forward in fear to the changes of life,
rather look to them with full hope that as they
arise, God will lead you safely through all things.
And when you cannot stand it,
God will carry you in His arms.
Do not fear what will happen tomorrow.
The same God who cares for you today
will take care of you today and every day.
God will either shield you from suffering or
will give you unfailing strength to bear it.
Be patient and put aside all anxious thoughts and
imaginations.

365
Humility

Humility is perpetual quietness of heart. It is to
have no trouble. It is never to be worried or angered,
irritable or distressed, to wonder at nothing that is
done to me, to feel nothing done against me. It is
to be at rest when nobody praises me, and when I
am blamed or despised; it is to have a blessed home
in myself where I can go in and shut the door and
kneel to my Father in secret and be at peace, as in
a deep sea of calmness, when all around and about
seems troubled.

Inscription on Dr. Bob's desk plaque, author unknown

366
I Try to Help People

I try to help people . . . experience their spiritual
connectedness by helping them get in touch with
both their tenderness and their power. I don't think
there's such a thing as instant intimacy or instant
spirituality—they are things that evolve in us. To
reach them . . . we need to see that . . . we are born

to evolve . . . It is a growing thing—and there is no fear in it. Not that we haven't heard the message before. It's what Christ talked about, and the Buddha, and others. But in the past most of us . . . said, "They're beyond us, they're divine . . . we're nothing but humans, so we can't make the same connection." But now, we're beginning to know we can.

Author unknown

References

Alcoholics Anonymous. 4th ed. New York: Alcoholics Anonymous World Services, 2001.

Beattie, Melody. *The Language of Letting Go.* Center City, MN: Hazelden, 1990.

A Day at a Time: Daily Reflections for Recovering People. Center City, MN: Hazelden, 1989.

The Little Red Book. Rev. ed. Center City, MN: Hazelden, 1986.

Twenty-Four Hours a Day. Rev. ed. Center City, MN: Hazelden, 1975.

Touchstones: A Book of Daily Meditations for Men. 2nd ed. Center City, MN: Hazelden, 1991.

Hazelden Foundation, a national nonprofit organization founded in 1949, helps people reclaim their lives from the disease of addiction. Built on decades of knowledge and experience, Hazelden's comprehensive approach to addiction addresses the full range of individual, family, and professional needs, including addiction treatment and continuing care services for youth and adults, publishing, research, higher learning, public education, and advocacy.

A life of recovery is lived "one day at a time." Hazelden publications, both educational and inspirational, support and strengthen lifelong recovery. In 1954, Hazelden published *Twenty-Four Hours a Day*, the first daily meditation book for recovering alcoholics, and Hazelden continues to publish works to inspire and guide individuals in treatment and recovery, and their loved ones. Professionals who work to prevent and treat addiction also turn to Hazelden for evidence-based curricula, informational materials, and videos for use in schools, treatment programs, and correctional programs.

Through published works, Hazelden extends the reach of hope, encouragement, help, and support to individuals, families, and communities affected by addiction and related issues.

For questions about Hazelden publications, please call 800-328-9000 or visit us online at hazelden.org/bookstore.